Anne Ablay
Peter Goulden
Neil Nuckley
Peter Toft

Oxford University Press

ABOUT THIS BOOK

This book will help you to think about images and the way they are presented as you design and make things.

Why do we design and make? Well, there are at least three answers to this question.

- Sometimes we design and make something to *solve a problem*.
- Sometimes we design and make because we see an opportunity to *produce something useful or valuable*.
- And sometimes we design and make *for fun*, just because we feel like it.

You can do all three as you work through this book. As you do so, you will need to work in certain ways including:

- thinking hard about a task or a problem;
- finding out or doing *research*;
- developing ideas;
- making;
- testing what you have made.

The book is divided into four sections.

- COMPANIES looks at the 'science of selling' and how companies present images to you.
- DISPLAYS looks at the changes that have taken place in how products are designed and sold.
- PACKAGING looks at different forms of packaging now and in the past.
- IMAGES looks at presentation and display. The last part of the section looks at the developing European Community.

In each section, you will find a number of topics. From each topic you will learn certain ideas and facts. You will also be asked to do certain tasks. Please note that you must always check with your teacher before starting these. To help you to recognise the different tasks, we have used symbols:

- ★ means *do* something;
- ■ means here is a useful *hint*;
- ◆ means you need to *find something out* or do research;
- ● means you are asked to think about or *discuss* something in class;
- ▲ means you need to *test* something out.

Designing and making things are important. So are thinking about packaging and presentation. But these are not the only reasons for this book. Designing and making things can be great fun. We hope you enjoy having such fun with the help of this book.

Anne Ablay   Peter Goulden   Neil Nuckley   Peter Toft

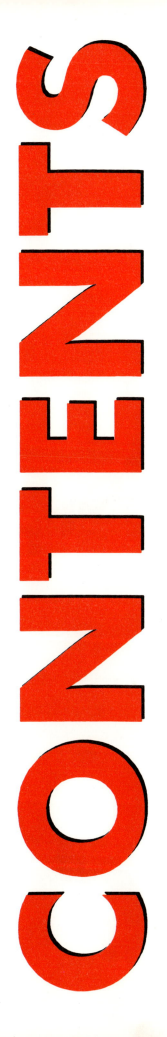

COMPANIES

6 Attracting the customer
8 Company identity
10 A design group in action

DISPLAYS

14 Changing displays
16 Designing a point of sale display
18 Support card graphics
20 Suspension packaging
22 Display unit design

PACKAGING

26 Packaging products
28 Packaging the way our ancestors did
30 Functional packaging
32 Packaging for image and presentation
34 Nature as a design source
36 The consequences of packaging

IMAGES

40 Presenting your own image
42 Presenting your work
44 Displaying your work
46 Presenting an image in Europe

48 Index

design

Logos

Brainstorm

symbols

research

advert

This section is about the care that is taken in designing a company image. You will learn how the 'science of selling' is applied to persuade you to spend your money. You will discover how companies help you remember their names, how lettering styles can be matched to 'images', how design groups develop company logos or symbols, and how graphical design skills are used in a wide range of situations.

COMPANIES

products

ising

ATTRACTING THE CUSTOMERS

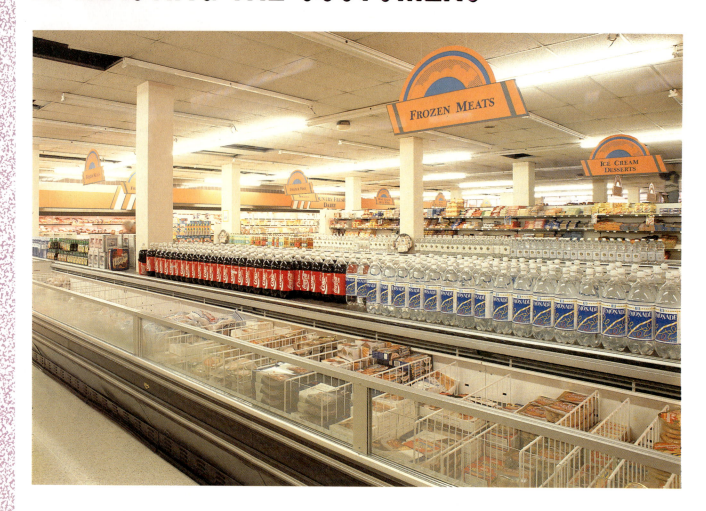

ADVERTISING

Supermarkets and shopping centres are carefully designed to attract customers and sell products. They offer us a chance to look at a wide range of skills and approaches that designers use in commerce and industry. Shops attempt to lure us towards them in different ways. They often advertise on television or in newspapers and magazines. Posters or signs are used along roads near a supermarket to display the company name and promote the goods it has on sale.

All of these ways of *advertising* will have been carefully designed to give information and to attract us with a welcoming 'image'. Before we even enter the supermarket this image will be presented to us in the design of the building and the colours of paintwork and signs.

The inside of a modern store will be designed to persuade you to spend as much money as possible. The displays are positioned to draw you in from the entrance. Careful lighting shows each display at its best. Often the smell of fresh baking will draw you into the far corner of the store. You will find that the most popular items are placed so that you can reach them easily without stretching.

In some supermarkets the sweets and confectionery are placed near to the floor and close to the check out point where harassed parents are often waiting with their children! The position of each display unit, the colours that are chosen for the decoration, the lighting, and the signs inside the supermarket have all been designed to encourage people to buy the products on display.

THE CUSTOMERS' SUPPORT TEAM

The supermarket will be designed to encourage us to return over and over again to spend our money. Getting the right atmosphere is important and everything that the customer sees must give the right 'image'. Of course, appearance must be linked to good service if the supermarket is to flourish. Three main skills are needed to make sure the customer gets good service. They are:

- good management;
- careful team work;
- thoughtful design.

Imagine shopping in a supermarket where staff were unhelpful or rude, the shelves dirty or the queues long. Would you go there again if a nearby supermarket offered better service?

Successful supermarkets are well managed. The staff work together as a team and often wear a uniform which helps to create team spirit and link the helpful attitude of the staff to the supermarket's image.

◆ Find out which supermarkets and restaurants in your area have staff uniforms to project the company image.

◆ Take a careful look at one of these uniforms. Does the design of the uniform match other design themes used on displays or products being sold?

DISPLAYS

Fruit, vegetables and even fish are often arranged to catch your eye and persuade you to buy. This is done quite deliberately. The displays are *designed* to attract the customer.

◆ Find out which are the most popular local supermarkets.

▲ Visit the store and look at the display of fresh vegetables. Consider how appealing it is. Make quick sketches or take photographs.

★ Back at home sketch the display. Use the sketch to show to your friends in class the methods used to make the display look attractive.

★ Make a labelled floor plan of the store to see if you can discover a pattern in the way that products are grouped. Where are the following: sweets, cigarettes, alcohol, vegetables, pet food, the bakery?

COMPANY IDENTITY

In a supermarket or a shop, many things that we see have been designed to link to the company's identity. To help us to remember the name of the company a 'symbol' or 'logo' is often used repeatedly in the displays or on printed materials. The logo is designed to be distinctive and easily remembered.

Consider a fast food restaurant. If we like what we have eaten there we may want to return. If the restaurant has a very clear image linked to a logo or made up into a sign, we will easily recognise it. We will then be likely to go in and spend more money there! Some companies try to make us recognise their sign by repeating it on a lot of their products, like the sign shown opposite.

◆ Think about a different kind of company, for instance a hotel chain. What symbol or logo does the company use to identify itself? Make a sketch of the logo.

SIGN LANGUAGE

In medieval times few people could read. Craft workers had to hang special signs outside their workshops. These signs or images helped customers to find the shops.

★ What kinds of shops do you think you would have found beneath these signs?

MEMORY

Some scientists have studied the way that we remember information. They have found that we remember visual images or simple pictures more easily than printed descriptions of those images.

★ Test your memory. Write down a list of words. Next to half the words draw a simple image that reminds you of the word, e.g. house.

★ Half an hour later write down all the words you can remember without looking at the list.

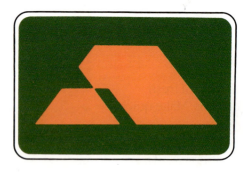

◆ Find out the names of the companies which use these symbols.

◆ Look through magazines to find other company symbols or logos. Either cut them out and paste into your note book or make simple outline sketches. Test your friends to see which ones they have seen and remembered.

DESIGN TASKS

Many companies link their names to visual symbols of the products or services they sell. Companies make these links so that their customers remember them more easily. The symbol is often linked to the product so that it both describes its appearance and suggests other qualities. 'Puma' training shoes for instance could have a symbol that looks like a puma and suggests the speed and power of the cat through its design.

★ Design suitable symbols or logos for these companies:

Electra Batteries;
Splash Swimming Goggles;
Sprint Running Shoes;
Swish Wrist Watches.

The lettering style used in magazines, posters, comics, and books is chosen very carefully to maintain the overall 'image' throughout. A lettering style used for medieval manuscripts would look out of place in a book on physics.

★ Look inside a catalogue of transfer lettering. You will find hundreds of different lettering styles. Some examples are shown opposite.

● Imagine you are opening a new shop selling either modern knitwear or model racing cars. Which lettering style would you choose from the catalogue to match the image you have of each? Why?

★ You can design your own style of lettering quite easily. Draw six faint parallel lines, then work out your letter shapes within them.

★ Design lettering styles which create these images: *expensive*; *fast*; *modern*.

★ Design a style of lettering for a motorbike courier service called CHEETAH.

Computers and their printers often have a wide range of lettering styles or *typefaces*. These are often called *founts*. You may find out about these by reading a manual for a computer or printer.

● Print five different typefaces and discuss with your friends the images each one has.

★ Find a typeface which matches one of the visual images you designed earlier. Use it to print the company name. Cut this out and paste it onto the drawing sheet to create a combined name and image.

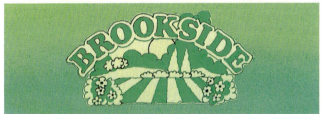

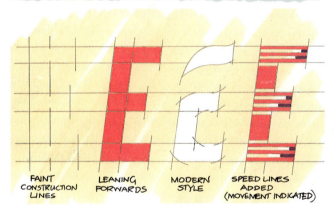

A DESIGN GROUP IN ACTION

When some companies have a design problem they often bring designers together to work in a *design group* to create a wide range of solutions.

THE TASK

Here is a newly-designed portable communicator. It can receive short messages for display on screen, and speech over long distances. It is small enough to slip into a pocket or handbag. The company which is marketing this new communicator wants to create a friendly but modern image for its products. Some techniques the design group might use in this task are: brainstorming; graphics; market research; mock-ups.

BRAINSTORMING

This could be used to find names for the communicator. We often say that "two heads are better than one". This means that it is often better for a group of people to try to solve a problem than for individuals to work alone. In *brainstorming*, a group of people try to think up and share ideas. One person's idea can trigger off a lot of further ideas in the other people's heads.

TRY IT YOURSELF

★ Try brainstorming to think up these names yourself. Work in groups of four or five. To be successful you need to use these hints.

■ Be clear about what you want to achieve.
■ Do not be afraid of putting ideas forward, even if they seem odd or silly. Sometimes today's silly idea can be tomorrow's solution.
■ Do not criticise or laugh at other people's ideas or they may get embarrassed. This could stop good ideas coming out into the open.
■ Practice – brainstorming does get easier. Write down or draw the ideas as they are spoken and let the whole group see them.

MARKET RESEARCH

The chosen names would be checked to see that they do not belong to another company and then tested on customers to find out which they liked best. This testing is called *market research*.

▲ Carry out a survey of your product names to find out how much others like them and why they like them.

LINKING THE NAME TO AN IMAGE

When the design group has found a suitable name for the communicator they may try to link an image to the name and so produce a symbol or logo that will be remembered easily. Simple designs are easier to remember than complex ones.

★ Try making quick outline drawings of symbols that could be linked to these names.

Visionquick   Communipad   Datascreen

■ Can you make these into symbols that use the letters from the name, yet still have a link with the image of the communicator?

The illustration opposite shows how the company symbol was developed and simplified. We call this process *abstraction*. This approach can help us to design symbols or logos.

■ Look for interesting shapes. Sketch them or paste pictures into your book. Use them to *abstract* images.

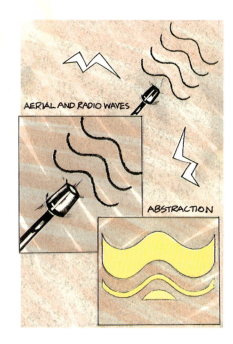

Colour

You can use colour to change a message and make a more powerful image. Designers will often experiment with a range of colours on the same design. To avoid having to repeat the design over and over again you can use a photocopier. Simply colour in your photocopies.

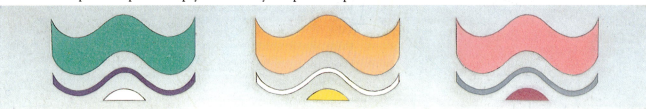

Mock-ups

Once suitable logos or symbols have been designed they will be tried out on various items like packaging, carrier bags, and stationery. These *mock-ups* will then be tried out on customers, and the company executives who are paying for the design. If the customers or the company do not like them, the design group must rethink their ideas.

■ Collect items linked to the same product, for example packaging, envelopes, and notepaper. Mount a display to show how the company projects its image.

A new company wants to start selling healthy, sugar-free sweets for young children.

Work in a small group to develop the following:
● a product name;
● an image for the company;
● a symbol to be used for advertising and sweet wrappers.

Try to 'sell' your final designs in a display to the rest of your class.

products

units

Bubble pack

Lighting

templates

support

DISPLAYS

In this section you will look at the changes that are taking place in the way many products are designed and sold. You will discover a number of different methods used for packaging and displaying products on suspension cards. You can also design and make your own suspension card system for a range of products and make a display stand to test out your design.

card *shrink wrap*

CHANGING DISPLAYS

In the past many shops displayed their goods on shelves behind the counter. The customer had to ask for each item. Then the shopkeeper collected them together and added up the bill. Shelves were often filled right up to the ceiling to make use of all the wall space. Sometimes the shopkeeper used a small pair of step-ladders to reach the top shelves.

★ Think about this kind of shopping. Discuss it with your parents. List its advantages and disadvantages for both the customer and the shopkeeper.

◆ Find out how shop design has changed. A comparison between your local corner shop and a high street supermarket will give you an idea of design changes.

DISPLAY CARDS

Recently, in many shops, products have been mounted on cardboard. The cardboard was then hung on a wall or rack and this saved valuable shelf space. Designers quickly realised that such cards could also be used to give advertising messages about the product.

★ Look carefully at some examples of this kind of display. Carry out the following tasks.

◆ What happens to the cardboard when all the products have been sold?

◆ Compare the price of the products sold in this way with the price of the same products sold in bulk.

★ List the advantages and disadvantages of selling products this way to the customer.

POINT OF SALE DISPLAYS

Suspended display units, like the one shown here, save space just like the display-card system. However, they can also be refilled with new products. You will often find this kind of display near the tills in modern stores, where it is sometimes called *a point of sale display*.

◆ Find a store near you which uses point of sale displays. Investigate the materials used and the ways in which products are held and displayed. Present your findings as notes and sketches.

DESIGNING A POINT OF SALE DISPLAY

CREATING WEALTH

Modern societies rely on industries which create wealth. The wealth can then be used to pay for services like schools and hospitals, as well as to give a good standard of living. Industries create wealth when they sell goods at a profit. Goods should sell better if they are:

- well designed;
- made to the right quality;
- carefully marketed.

Part of the marketing of goods is a well-designed display. The last page introduced *point of sale displays*. We are now going to examine these more closely.

◆ Find a book on business studies and examine how companies market goods and make profits.

● Look carefully at the confectionery shop above. Discuss your opinions about the success of the shop in these areas: *attractiveness to you*; *colour*; *ease of use*; *image*; *lighting*.

DESIGN TASK

★ Design and make a point of sale display unit, with labels and packaging, for a range of personal care products. Examples of these products are shown on the left and the design process is broken down into easy stages to help you.

DESIGN CONSTRAINTS

The sales unit should fit into the sizes shown opposite. It will either be clipped to the end of a row of shelves or be used next to other display units in general stores.

◆ Investigate the kinds of images that young people find attractive. Talk to your friends and look at teenage magazines. Look at a magazine which is out of date and compare it with a modern one.

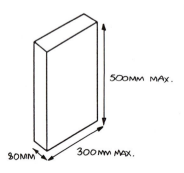

16

PRESENTING A PRODUCT IMAGE

Image is very important in selling personal care products. Every part of your display system should present an image which people find attractive.

★ Use brainstorming to create a range of product names.

★ Try to choose a name that would work in Europe as well as the UK. We are now having to design for a single European market and language skills will become more important.

★ Carry out a survey of friends to evaluate the success of these names.

★ Design styles of lettering and visual images to match your chosen names.

LABELLING THE PRODUCTS

★ Design and make labels that present the image you have chosen. You can model the labels on used containers by carefully sticking the new label over the old product name. Plastic containers can be resprayed to the colour of your choice with a car spray or air marker.

■ Computer graphics can give a wide range of lettering styles.
■ Designs drawn onto sticky-back labels and cut to size can produce a very professional finish.
■ Many computer printers can print onto these sticky-back labels.

DESIGNING A SUPPORT CARD

The support card slots are all made to the same *standard* size. This is shown below. Do not forget to allow space for these slots in your graphical design when planning the card!

Your personal care products can be held on to the support card in various ways.

◆ Investigate the different ways in which products can be held onto support cards by collecting a wide range of used cards. Present your findings as notes and sketches.

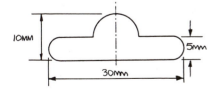

SUPPORT CARD GRAPHICS

If your support card is to convey your intended message, its layout, image, and colour need to be designed with care. Consider the following:

■ Will any graphics or lettering be hidden when the product is on the card?

■ What information should the card give about the product?

■ Will there be a price label on the card? Where will it be placed?

CREATING A RANGE OF IDEAS

★ Mark out a series of product card outlines on sheets of layout paper. Experiment with different sizes of product, different layouts, and different images to make sure that all elements of the design work well together.

USING A PHOTOCOPIER

At this stage you can save a lot of time if you can use a photocopier.

★ Choose the most effective of your design ideas. Make a *master copy* for printing on the photocopier. This master copy should be as good as you can make it so that your copies are of good quality. Avoid large areas of black and thick lines. Many photocopiers will copy these unevenly. Follow the machine instructions carefully.

■ First draw a faint line in pencil.
■ Draw in your design using a technical pen and black ink.
■ Use white correcting fluid if you make a mistake.
■ Dry transfer lettering can look professional when copied.
■ *Most* dry transfer lettering copies well.
■ If you want an area of heavy line, try hatching using a technical pen with a thinner nib.
■ Dry transfer shading can be used to shade large areas.
■ If you stick paper onto the master the lines around it can show up black on the copy. To avoid this, place document repair tape along the joins.

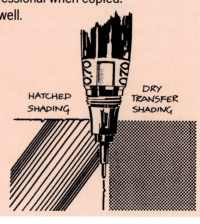

USING COLOUR FOR IMPACT

You can use colour to improve your design in many ways. Experiment with different techniques to see their effects. For these experiments use photocopies of your design or tracings made on layout paper.

Pencil crayons

These are very effective for subtle rather than bold designs. To get the best results use them as shown here.

■ Use long, even strokes with gentle pressure over the whole area.

■ Move the crayon in one direction only.

■ If you want to lighten the colour or remove it, use a soft plastic rubber.

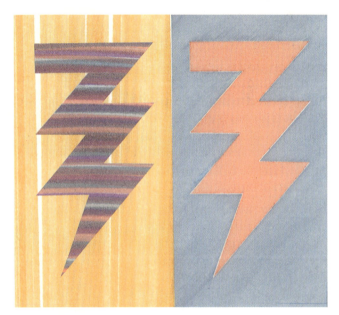

Marker pens

■ These can be used to give strong, bold effects. Be careful though, as they can quickly ruin your work if used badly. Markers often leave a *striped* effect. You can make this look even by using a ruler as a guide when colouring over an area. If you want to avoid this striped effect work quickly to keep the ink wet.

■ Test your marker on the paper you want to colour to make sure the effect is right. Also check whether the marker *bleeds* right through the paper. If it does, put paper below your design.

■ Studio markers have a very wide range of colours and shades.

■ Plastic tape can be used to *mask* areas that you do not want to colour. Be careful that the colour does not *run* under the tape.

Other effects

You can get lots of other different colour effects, some of which are shown below. A mask or *template* may help you to apply the colour exactly where you want it.

SPATTER

DIFFUSER

AIR MARKER

SUSPENSION PACKAGING

By now, you should know that many products are sold on suspended cards. They need to be fastened securely to the card until the customer has bought them. If they are not secure they may move about on the card and suffer damage, especially when being transported.

OPTIONS

1 A very simple but effective package can be provided by fastening a small plastic bag to a suspension card using staples.

2 The product is held onto the card by a thin plastic film. The film is heated to make it expand. Then it is placed onto the card where it cools and shrinks. This shrinkage makes the film hold the product in place. We call this *shrink wrapping*.

3 Here the product for sale is simply attached to the card by pushing it through a slot. The clip is closed and held securely to the card.

4 This cardboard box has been cut and folded with a long back flap to allow it to be used on suspension displays. The transparent window allows you to see the product inside.

◆ Can you find examples of darning wools, ribbon, elastic or cotton thread that are sold on suspension displays? What systems have been used to hold these materials?

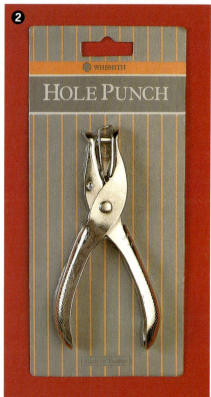

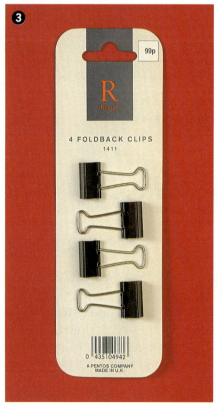

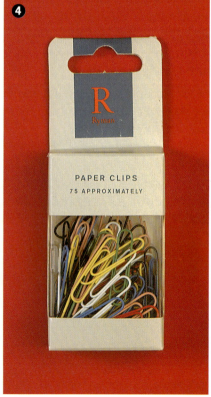

BUBBLE PACKAGING

More and more products are sold in *bubble packs*. These are strong plastic shells fixed onto the suspension card. The bubble holds, displays, and protects the contents. Bubble packs can display larger items than *shrink wrapping*.

◆ Visit local shops and supermarkets. Make notes and sketches of other types of suspension card.

● Discuss the effects of this kind of packaging on the price customers pay for the products. What advantages does this type of packaging have for the customer and the retailer? Are there any disadvantages?

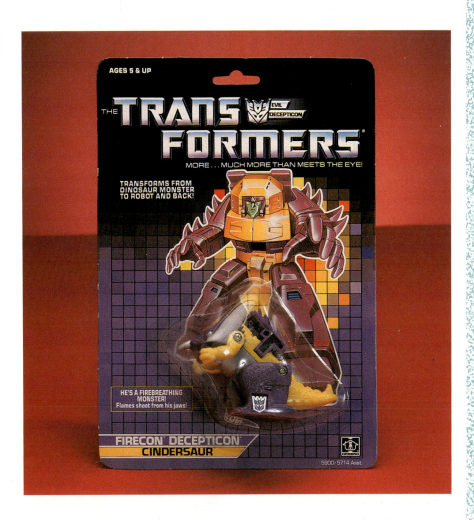

MAKING A BUBBLE PACK WITH A VACUUM FORMING MACHINE

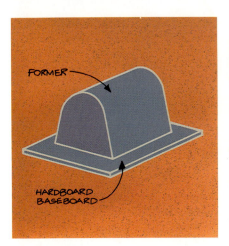

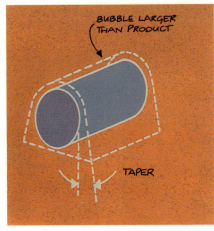

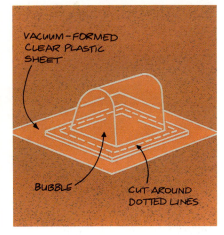

You need to make a mould slightly larger than the product. It must have a slight taper or *draught* to allow the mould to slide out of the formed plastic.

Use an easily worked material such as jellutong or medium density fibreboard. Bring it to a good finish with glasspaper.

Vacuum form the bubble. Trim any waste using scissors. Cut round a template if you are making a few to the same size. Join the bubble to the card with clear glue or double-sided tape.

DISPLAY UNIT DESIGN

There are various kinds of display unit in many places such as shops, supermarkets, banks, post offices, and petrol stations. Some are shown here.

1 *Carousel units* which rotate can be used where floor space is short, or in odd corners on a counter.

2 These units have back panels made of *peg-board*. The board has holes cut in a regular pattern for hooks to slot into. The hooks can be moved and so displays can be changed quickly.

3 Where there is a small area of unused wall space, display panels can be mounted at eye level.

◆ Look carefully at the display units in local chemists and supermarkets. Make notes and sketches to record how they are made and how the cards are held.

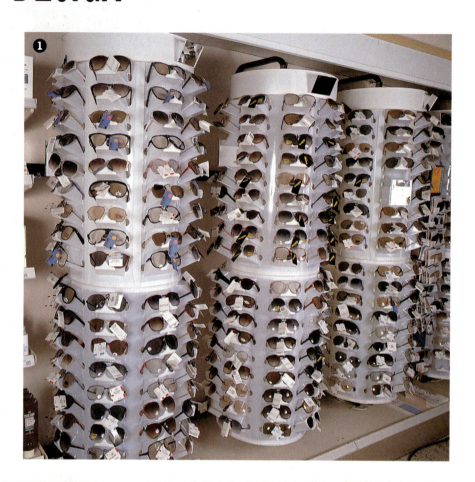

DESIGN TASK: A DISPLAY UNIT FOR YOUR PERSONAL CARE PRODUCTS

Consider where and how the unit would be located. Bear the following in mind.

■ What *image* will the stand project?

■ How many cards will it display?

■ Will the cards be different?

■ How big will the cards be?

■ Will a *header panel* giving the product name be used?

■ Should the colour of the display stand link up with the cards?

■ How will the suspension hangers be made? Strong metal wire is one solution.

★ Develop your design idea with sketches, drawings and a cardboard *mock-up*. When you have reached a satisfactory solution, make a full-sized *prototype*.

▲ Evaluate your model – discuss it in a group. Consider the following: *image*; *access* to the cards; *displaying* the products; ease of *making*; *space* needed for the unit.

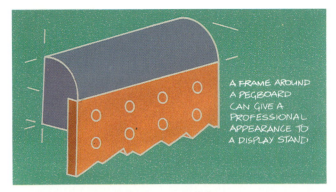

A FRAME AROUND A PEGBOARD CAN GIVE A PROFESSIONAL APPEARANCE TO A DISPLAY STAND

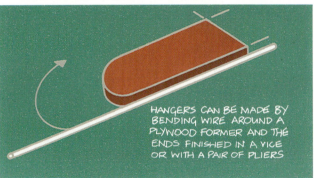

HANGERS CAN BE MADE BY BENDING WIRE AROUND A PLYWOOD FORMER AND THE ENDS FINISHED IN A VICE OR WITH A PAIR OF PLIERS

TEAM TASK: MINI-ENTERPRISE PROJECT (1)

Designers play a vital role in helping producers to sell at a profit. However, they are only part of a team that attempts to balance the needs of manufacturers with those of consumers. To find out more about how a business is run, set up a mini-enterprise company in your own school. You will have to decide yourselves what products you want to sell or manufacture. School businesses have ranged from plant propagation and Christmas card painting to small scale manufacturing. Your Business Studies teacher may be able to offer advice on how to get started. Try to sell your products at a profit and use these profits to help the school or a charity.

Warning

All of the benefits of good design have a cost.

Packaging is criticised because it *wastes resources*, *creates litter*, and *increases product price*.

● Consider these issues and discuss them with your friends. The arguments can be very complicated and can form an interesting topic for a written assignment.

graphics

Boxes

Recycling

Style

materials

cost

This section deals with the different functions of packaging. You will learn about packaging in the past, commercial packaging, functional packaging, and packaging for image and presentation. The consequences of packaging and using nature as a design source for packaging are considered. The section also includes starting points which you may find useful for your design and make projects.

modules

mechanisms

PACKAGING

PACKAGING PRODUCTS

Packaging is the name we use for all kinds of containers in which products are packed for consumers.

● Think about all the different ways of packaging these products.

food	cosmetics	games
drink	toiletries	electrical goods
medicines	clothes	DIY items

Here are some examples. Can you think of any more?

GRAPHICS

Most packages tell us about their contents by use of *graphics*. Graphics include different kinds of drawing and lettering to describe a product in pictures and words. They are designed to attract our attention and make us want to buy them, as well as telling us about the product. Usually they show the maker's name and company image.

▲ What image do you think this package is designed to show? Is it successful?

COSTS

The new methods of packaging and display aimed at consumers not only bring us benefits. They also have a cost. Often we fail to predict or bother about some of these costs.

Packages have recently become throwaway items. Even packages which look attractive and expensive in shops are thrown away.

This can be ugly and dangerous as our surroundings become littered with used packages. Some packages, such as milk bottles, are re-used. However, most are not and are thrown away.

PACKAGING THE WAY OUR ANCESTORS DID

Our prehistoric ancestors gradually spread over the world's surface. They settled in warm fertile valleys and plains, on mountains and in deserts, swamps and forests, or by rivers and seas. Each group of people developed its own customs to suit where it lived. Some hunted, gathered and fished, others farmed or kept herds of animals.

All these groups needed vessels to carry, wrap and store their possessions in. Our ancestors of 5000 years ago could not buy plastic bags or cardboard boxes. They had to use the natural resources available where they lived.

● Identify as many natural resources as you can in the picture above which could be used for packaging.

DESIGN TASK: PACKAGING USING NATURAL PRODUCTS

● Discuss in small groups what each of the following groups of people would need to carry and store to survive:

   herders; farmers; fishers; hunter-gatherers.

◆ Using words or sketches make a list of containers and wrapping materials which they might *find in their surroundings*. Use library books and talk to friends and teachers about this.

★ Choose one natural container or wrapping material that you can get hold of. Use it to make a package to store one of the following:

   water;   clothes;   cosmetics;
   food;   jewellery;   dyes;
   weapons;   items of worship;   tools.

If you live in the city or cannot easily find these raw materials, think of some alternatives. You could weave with paper or fabric strips, or mould containers from papier mâché.

★ Decorate the finished package with a design to show others that the contents are *precious*. Use drawings only – no words.

● Do you think these containers and wrappings were meant to be thrown away? Do you think they would create litter problems?

◆ One advantage of natural packaging is that it is *biodegradable*. Find out what this means. Why is it an advantage?

COMMERCIAL PACKAGING

When groups living far apart began to trade with one another packaging changed. Products had to be kept safe during long journeys over land or sea. To meet this need *commercial packaging* was developed.

Before it could develop, groups had to be able to make lots of packages well. People also had to be able to read what was printed on them.

The first manufacturers known to have packaged their products were German papermakers. In the early eleventh century they used their own fine paper, decorated with printed designs, to wrap up the paper they sold.

★ Go to your local newsagent or gift shop. Make a list of all the different wrapping papers they sell.

★ Design your own wrapping paper and gift tag using a repeating pattern.

MINI-ENTERPRISE PROJECT (2)

Well-designed packaging helps to sell the contents. Design your own containers and labels to package products which you have made yourself. You could sell your products at a school fair and help your school fund or a charity.

Here are some ideas you might consider.

■ Package pins in the Victorian style.

■ Package biscuits you have made yourself. Try to make the package look 'wholesome', 'country fresh' or 'home-baked'.

■ Design exotic packets for spices, herbs or pulses.

■ Package a small DIY kit.

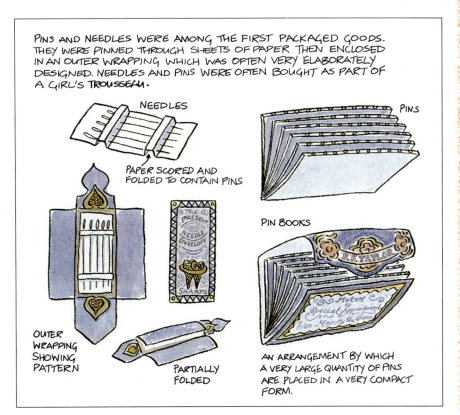

FUNCTIONAL PACKAGING

There was little demand for commercial packaging in Britain until the end of the eighteenth century. In 1794 the population was under 9 million and few people could read. A few packages did exist though. These were made and printed by hand, which took a very long time. Even the paper, from which some packages were made, had to be made by hand.

By the end of the eighteenth century paper could be made by machine and printed with coloured designs by machine. This made packaging much cheaper and more useful for industry, especially at first in America.

★ Experiment with hand printing and produce your own patterned paper.

STICK AN EXPANDED POLYSTYRENE BLOCK OR TILE TO A PIECE OF HARDBOARD USING PVA GLUE. ALLOW 4 HOURS DRYING TIME. WHEN DRY, TURN OVER, DRAW THE DESIGN ONTO THE TILE WITH A FELT TIP PEN.

PAINT OVER THE AREAS WHICH WILL PRINT THE DESIGN WITH A THICK EMULSION PAINT.

IF YOU BEGIN WITH A SIMPLE SOLID SHAPE PRINTED IN A PALE COLOUR YOU CAN CUT AWAY MORE OF THE DESIGN AND PRINT AGAIN IN A DARKER COLOUR ADDING DETAIL. LETTERING CAN BE APPLIED WITH LETRASET.

CUT AWAY THE WHITE AREAS TO A DEPTH OF APPROXIMATELY 5MM WITH A SMALL HOT WIRE CUTTER. THE PRINTED AREA WILL NOT BE AFFECTED.

COAT THE RAISED DESIGN WITH A CREAMY LAYER OF EMULSION OR PRINTING INK APPLIED WITH A ROLLER.
LAY A SHEET OF PAPER OVER THE BLOCK AND ROLL AGAIN WITH A CLEAN ROLLER.

During the nineteenth century some shopkeepers continued to package their own goods but most stopped. Big manufacturers packaged their products themselves. For this they needed new machines, not just to make the packaging, but to weigh out their contents, fill the packets and seal them.

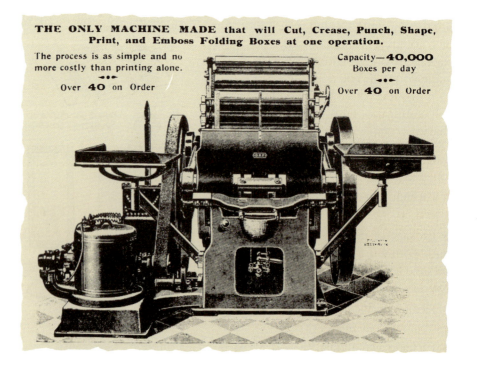

DESIGN TASK: WOOD AND CARDBOARD BOXES

A matchbox is a functional package. It holds matches securely and gives a surface to strike them on. Matchbox design has changed little over the years.

The box is the most widely used form of packaging. Early boxes, for example pill boxes, were made of wood. Wood was not suitable for printing on. The graphic design was printed on paper which was then stuck on to the box. In the twentieth century most boxes have been made from cardboard.

◆ Go to your local supermarket and look at packaging which has labels stuck on and packaging which is directly printed on.

★ Collect labels for your design book.

Ultra-slick card cosmetic packages.

Modern card boxes are designed in many shapes and sizes. Some rely on graphics for impact, and some rely on their unusual forms and clever *cardboard engineering*.

Easter egg boxes are good examples. They come in all shapes and sizes. They are cleverly engineered to show off and protect the eggs. They are also covered in exciting images and colours.

★ Collect some different types of cardboard packages.

★ Carefully open them up. Study how they have been made. Look at the difference between the flat, opened-up pattern and the 3-D made-up form.

How many surfaces are used for gluing?

Does the graphic design suit the form of the box?

★ Design and make a box for a new sweet or snack of your own invention. Here are some ideas to start you off:

    hyperspacers;   popsters;
    robot fuel;   inter-stellar meteor munchies.

Consider the graphic design together with the form of the box. Create the image you feel best suits the new sweet or snack.

Work out your ideas on paper. Test your ideas on classmates to find which is the most popular. Make the final design and work with the rest of your group to make a display of all the boxes produced.

■ To make clean folds, *score* the card along the creases. Do this by drawing the cutting edge of a pair of scissors along the crease, guided by a steel rule, just as you would draw a ruled pencil line. Be careful not to cut right through the card.

PACKAGING FOR IMAGE AND PRESENTATION

Have you ever heard the expression "She's as pretty as a picture?" Look at these illustrations and you will understand why this expression was used.

Images are often used to make us want to buy the box, not necessarily the contents! Turn on the TV and see how often attractive people are used to sell cars, sweets, drinks . . .

Some of the most decorative metal containers were used by Huntley and Palmer in the nineteenth century. They were airtight and contained biscuits. Most found a place on mantelpieces and shelves long after the biscuits were eaten.

TIN CANS

The biscuit containers were made from tin-plate. Tin-plate is actually steel coated with a thin layer of tin. The steel provides strength and the tin covering stops the steel *corroding*. Manufacturers of tin-plate quickly realised that these airtight containers were ideal for the preservation of solid food. The canned food industry started as far back as 1824.

John Gamble packed roast veal into cans for Parry's voyage in search of the north-west passage. The instructions on the paper label read as follows: *"Cut round the top near the outer edge with a chisel and hammer"*.

It appears that cans were invented before anyone thought of the can-opener!

Unlike the decorative biscuit tins which were kept as ornaments, food cans were and are thrown away when empty.

DESIGN TASK

★ Design and make a luxury package which someone will want to keep. Discuss this with your teacher then write your own design brief. You will need to consider these points.

■ Research
What will it hold?
Who will it be for?
What kinds can you see in the shops which you would like to keep?
Will it be for everyday use or just for special occasions?

■ Style
What form do you want the package to take?
Do you want it to be *exciting*, *simple*, *beautiful*, *elegant*, *functional*, etc.?

■ Mechanism
How do you want the box to open?
Will there be a sliding or a hinged lid?
Will it open with a secret catch?
Will there be a hidden drawer?

■ Material
Sometimes the actual materials will suggest starting points for designing. Sometimes the most suitable materials are not chosen until a lot of designing has been done. Here are some materials to consider.

MATERIALS

Different types of card – corrugated, smooth, shiny, thick, thin, coloured, modelling card (a layer of polystyrene foam sandwiched between two layers of card).

Acrylics – sheet, rod, tube, clear and coloured, laminated (different layers stuck together).

Polystyrene – the high impact sheet which is good for vacuum forming.

Wood – plywood, veneers (plain or stained), jellutong.

Metals – copper, brass, gilding metal.

Textiles – velvet, satin, silk.

Each of these materials will require different types of adhesive. Check what is available with your teacher.

FINISHES

You can choose from a number of finishes.

■ Card
Print a pattern using a polystyrene printing block and emulsion paint.
Use felt tips.
Add a collage of different papers – foil, sticky, tissue, etc.
Spray with a diffuser or air marker.
Use marbling techniques.
The surface patterns on the card boxes can be protected by adding a layer of clear sticky-backed plastic.

■ Acrylic
Dye clear acrylic.
Cut shapes into one coloured sheet and place behind another.
Engrave.

■ Wood
Draw a design with felt tips then varnish.
Burn a design with a pyrograph.
Sandblast or wire brush the surface.
Add a design in veneers.

NATURE AS A DESIGN SOURCE

Most packaging containers are developed from basic geometrical shapes such as the square, rectangle and circle. In industry, many objects are made to exactly the same shape and size. This is called *mass production*. Mass production is easier if the machines can be adapted to the exact size and shape of the product. Regular geometrical shapes are best for this. Also, regular shapes can be stacked closely together. This saves space (and money) when packages are being transported.

● Packages based on triangles and pyramids are not often used. Why do you think this is? How could triangular boxes be packed together?

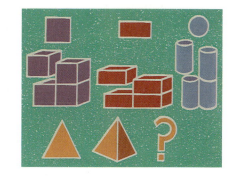

NATURAL GEOMETRY

You might think that regular geometrical shapes have been invented by people. If you did you would be wrong! Many geometrical designs were borrowed from natural objects which have *geometric* form.

◆ Examine some natural forms very closely. Your naked eye might be suitable or you may need to use a magnifying glass or microscope. Occasionally, studying photographs will be enough. You will see that many natural forms contain row after row of nearly perfect geometrical shapes. Some are much more complicated than circles and squares.

★ Make a collection of drawings of the natural forms you have examined. Here are some examples for you to study:
    a selection of leaves;   shells;
    the stems of plants;   microscopic cells;
    winged insects;   minerals or crystals.

MODULES

When a number of similar shapes are used together, we call them *modules*. For example, the segments of a pine cone are similar to each other but not identical. They fit together to make the cone. The cone will also be different in shape to other cones on the tree.

★ Take one of the four modules shown opposite. Repeat it to create a pattern.

★ Use two or more of the modules to create a more complex pattern.

★ Design your own geometrical module and repeat it to form a pattern.

■ Use card *templates* of the basic modules to draw around.

★ Use your patterns to create: a 3-D structure; a container; surface decoration for wrapping paper.

★ You may be able to work out your modular patterns on a computer. Check with your teacher.

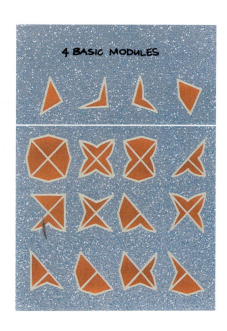

BUBBLES

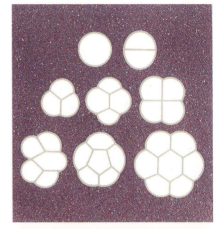

Examine soap bubbles. They can give you an interesting starting point for 3-D structures. When a single soap bubble floats freely it is spherical (ball-shaped). When bubbles are packed closely together, though, they change shape. They tend to fill up the empty spaces and take on different geometrical shapes.

★ Make some soap bubbles. Observe them closely. Carefully draw all the geometrical forms you can see.

★ Talk to your chemistry teacher about making a *bubble raft*. If you can, make one and use drawings or take photographs to show that the bubbles form patterns.

★ Talk to your mathematics teachers about *tessellations*. Look at some tessellations from the school mathematics rooms to see if they are similar to the soap bubbles.

★ Make 3-D models based on the soap bubble formations you have drawn. Work out ways of fitting the different modules together.

● When the models are finished, make a class display. Discuss each to judge its: *appearance*; *strength*; *stability*.

● How can your study of bubbles be used as a starting point to design and make *functional* (useful) packages? Discuss the following in small groups:

   a supermarket display unit;
   multipurpose storage for shops;
   packaging for fragile products;
   packaging for children's science fiction toys.

NATURE'S PACKAGES

Designers rarely invent straight from their imagination. Often they observe the rich world of human, animal and natural forms for ideas. Nature often produces ingenious packages. You can learn a lot by studying these.

Look at how plants package and protect their seeds. These shapes have *evolved* to make sure that the seeds spread out when they are ripe. Some catch the wind and some hook onto animals as they pass.

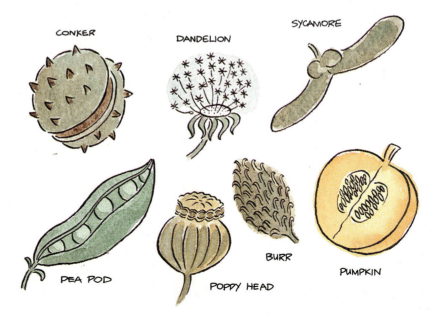

★ Collect nuts, berries, seed pods, and fruits. Cut them in half and draw the cross sections.

★ Design and make a container with a hidden surprise. Base your design on your drawings of "nature's packages".

THE CONSEQUENCES OF PACKAGING

Pollution of the environment by toxic waste, fumes, noise and litter is a major problem for industrialized countries. We also are using up the world's natural resources like forests and oil. All this so that we can buy and then throw away!

● Discuss with your teacher and classmates what life would be like today if previous generations had thrown away as much as we do. What will life be like in the future if we continue to throw away large amounts of rubbish?

RECYCLING USED MATERIALS

★ What can *we* do to make use of some of the packaging containers we throw away?

In some non-industrial countries, people treasure what we throw away. Think of some ways you could help to re-use what we think of as rubbish.
Could you use waste materials for modelling and making things in school?
Jot down ideas in your notebook for ways in which you might use: scrap metal; wrapping paper; cartons; boxes; bottles; polystyrene foam; fabrics.

▲ Investigate some of the ways used to separate rubbish into different re-useable types, e.g. glass bottles.

★ Fragile items are often packaged in boxes filled with *plastic granules* that are immediately thrown away. The granules might be useful. If packaged in something other than cardboard they could be moulded to fit different shapes. Use this idea to design a safe resting place for a fragile item.

USEFUL SCRAP

This picture shows the way poor but resourceful people have converted what we consider to be scrap – car number plates – into a useful item – a stove. It uses charcoal as a fuel but this is an increasingly scarce resource in many developing countries. The number plates are soldered together and the wire loops can be used to carry the stove short distances.

This radio receiver is made from a used fruit juice can. Its power source is paraffin wax and a wick. The heat is converted into energy to power the receiver. Dried cow dung and other substances can be used instead of wax. It was designed by Victor Papanek and George Seeger.

The same radio is shown here decorated with coloured felt cutouts and sea shells by a user in Indonesia. Local materials can be used creatively to disguise the fact that the radio is made from re-used materials.

DESIGN TASK

★ Form small brainstorming groups to carry out this task.

1 Make a list of all the throw-away waste products you know of.
2 Take promising items from this list and think up as many uses as you can for the waste material.

★ Starting with ideas created in this brainstorming, design and make something *useful* from what is considered to be *useless* waste.

Be careful because handling some waste items can be dangerous.
Remember that re-using materials like this will not solve the problem of depleting the world's resources. To do this we would need to *recycle* waste.

◆ Find out what *recycling* means.

quality

Teams

symmetry

Projects

exports

present

The first part of this section is about presentation and display. It contains useful tips on how to present your course work notes, assignments, presentation drawings, and models. It also gives information on how to put up a display and mount your graphics presentation work. Trading between the twelve European Community nations will be easier from 1992. The last part of this section of the book deals with the European Community and the roles designers, manufacturers, and the tourist industry might play within it.

PRESENTING YOUR OWN IMAGE

LAYOUT AND DESIGN

When an illustrated book such as this one is being developed, authors, editors, designers and illustrators work together to produce and refine the way a book is presented. Words, illustrations and photographs must all be linked within a good design to give the right *feel* for the book. When the layouts have been finalised, *proof* copies are produced which are carefully checked (see left).

COVERS

The first thing people see of a book is the cover. To market and sell books effectively, the cover should catch the eye and arouse interest in spite of all the competition. It should also express what the book is about. Book designers, like record sleeve designers, therefore pay particular attention to the cover in order to convey the right image for the book, by a careful balance of typography, illustrations and use of colour.

Photographs have to be chosen with care.

A special camera photographs line drawings at different sizes.

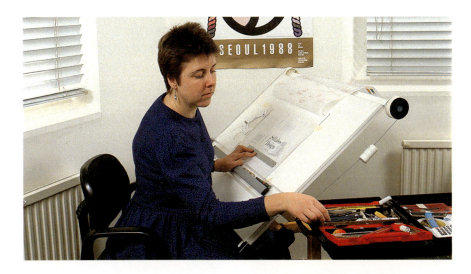

The artwork to be included in a book has to be selected carefully to fit in with the design. Drawings and photographs can be enlarged or reduced and cut in various ways to produce different effects. The type must be carefully pasted up in position before going to the printer (see left).

USING TECHNOLOGY

You may have access in your school to word processing and desk-top publishing equipment. This can give a very professional image to your work providing you think carefully about such things as layout, balance and typography.

★ In your next design task try presenting your work so that other readers can follow it.

PRESENTING YOUR WORK

QUALITY COUNTS

Our first impressions of people and things are very important. Clothes, pop groups and cars all have a carefully chosen appearance. They are designed to make a good first impression. Designers know just how important this image can be. They know that it is often worthwhile polishing, preparing and improving their work to improve that image.

Your projects give you the chance to give a carefully designed appearance to your work. This will enhance the original and creative effort of the project and attract interest. The image of your work can be a foundation for your own success and you should take it very seriously.

PRESENTING YOUR ASSIGNMENTS

First impressions also count in your assignments. A well designed cover is a great way to give a good impression.

If your assignment is on loose-leaved pages you might design and make a folder for them. This will give added protection, and may hold brochures and other useful information you have collected.

★ Write to local firms for samples of their brochures or conference folders.
Compare the images they present.
Do they have a company logo?
Open the folders to discover how they are made.

★ Try to use the best ideas from these brochures when designing your own folder.

COURSEWORK NOTES

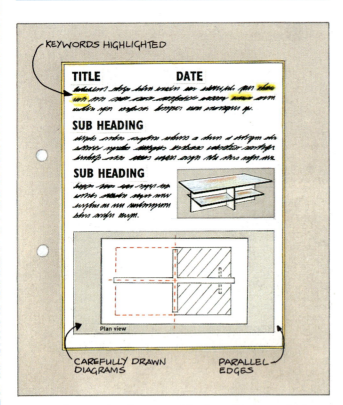

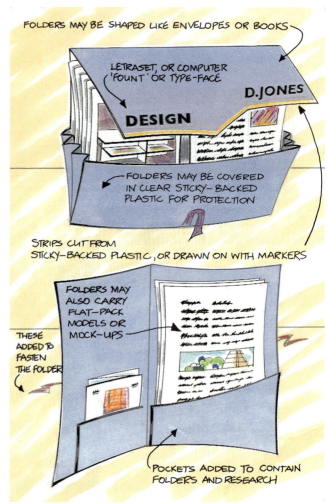

Neat and organised notes with clear diagrams help you to learn *and* give a good impression. Use enough space to present your work clearly and try to achieve a balance between illustrations and text.

PROJECT WORK

It is very important to keep all your design work to show how you have developed your ideas. A well-prepared project, carefully presented, will enable you to make a good impression and will help you gain marks.

IDEAS SHEET
IDEAS SHEETS SHOULD BE EXACTLY THAT; FULL OF IDEAS. NOT ONE OR TWO BUT LOTS. THEY NEED NOT BE TOTALLY DIFFERENT. ONE IDEA CAN LEAD ON FROM ANOTHER. ALL YOUR IDEAS ARE IMPORTANT AT THIS STAGE AND ALL MUST BE PUT ONTO PAPER — YOU CAN SELECT OUT LATER.

YOUR RESEARCH PAGE SHOULD BE LIVELY, FULL OF INFORMATION AND SHOW YOUR DEPTH OF UNDERSTANDING OF THE PROBLEM TO BE SOLVED. IT SHOULD ALSO SHOW VARIED SOLUTIONS.

SPECIFICATION

COVERS SHOULD PROTECT THE LOOSE-LEAFED PAGES. THIN MANILA CARD OR GOOD QUALITY PAPER SUITABLE HERE.

PLASTIC SPINE

LINE UP AND CAREFULLY SPACE OUT ANY ADDITIONAL WORK WHICH HAS TO BE STUCK DOWN.

MAKE SURE THE EDGES OF THE WORK ARE PARALLEL WITH THE EDGES OF THE MAIN SHEET.

DESIGN TASK: LOGO

★ Design a *logo* based on your initials to help create an identity symbol for your work.

★ Look through a catalogue of dry transfer lettering. Find a style that matches the logo you have designed. Do not forget to work out the positions of the letters before you stick them down.

★ Can you find a computer *fount* or typeface which suits your logo design?

43

DISPLAYING YOUR WORK

There will be times during the year when you are able to display your work to other pupils, visitors and parents. You may have to mount a display of your work for an examination.

You can show your coursework to best advantage by careful display. Spending time choosing and presenting your work – design folders, models, mock-ups, drawings and finished products – is always time well spent.

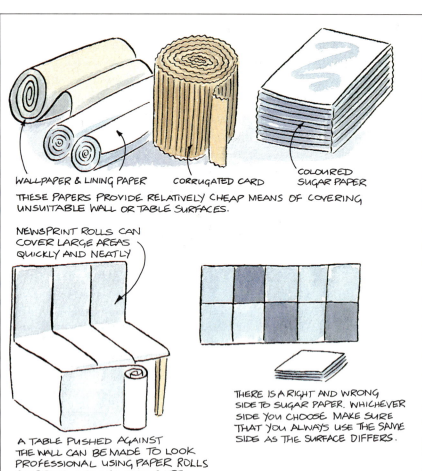

WALL-MOUNTED DISPLAYS

Wall-mounted displays are most suitable for your graphics work. It can be seen without much effort by the viewer.

Take care in choosing the work you will present like this as it hits the viewer's eye first. Remember the importance of first impressions. Place your best work to the centre of the panel with all linked drawings arranged around it. This will help to show how your ideas have developed.

You can present some 3-D work like this providing it is not too heavy.

You must choose a suitable background to display your work. Walls or display boards can become shabby very quickly. Overcome this by covering them with backing paper. Choose a colour which will show off your work to best advantage.

MOUNTING GRAPHICS WORK

You can *window mount* or *surface mount* your work. Whichever you choose you must consider these points.

■ Choose mounting paper or card which complements your work and does not clash with it.

■ Cut your work to size. Make sure corners are square and edges straight. Draw the shape you want to cut very lightly with an HB pencil, on the *back* of the work, using a metal rule or set square.

■ Cut with a craft knife and metal rule, or use a guillotine. Scissors are not suitable.

■ If you intend to stick your drawings onto the mounts use an adhesive which will not damage the paper. The surface of the paper will not be damaged if you make a mistake.

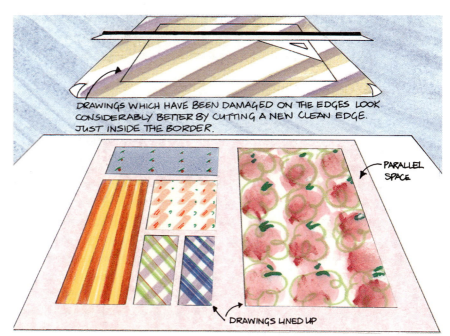

■ Be sure to stick your work down flat.

■ If you are mounting more than one drawing on the same mount, move the drawings around the sheet until you are satisfied with the arrangement. Line up the work. Pay particular attention to the sizes of the gaps between each piece, and to the borders, to achieve a good balance.

■ Try to achieve *symmetry* in your display.

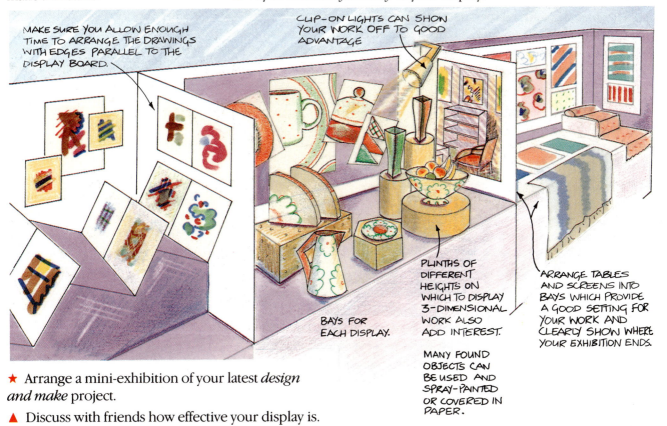

★ Arrange a mini-exhibition of your latest *design and make* project.

▲ Discuss with friends how effective your display is.

45

PRESENTING AN IMAGE FOR EUROPE

Many of the products designed in the U.K. are sold abroad. The *export* of products to other countries raises money which can be used to buy materials and goods from other countries. If we do not sell enough products we do not make enough money to buy what we need and a *trade gap* develops.

There are twelve countries in the European Community (EC). British companies have had difficulties designing products for these countries as each country has needed a separate version of each product. This creates a lot of extra work and cost for the producer.

After 1992 all this will have changed. For example, before this date a producer had to apply separately to ten different countries to get EC protection for other people copying designs. After 1992 only one application will be needed for protection in all twelve countries. The countries will also all agree on the same regulations for the design of products. Designers will therefore only have to design one version of a new product instead of twelve!

THE SINGLE MARKET

After 1992, there will be a single market in the EC with 320,000,000 possible customers. Companies who design, make, and sell high quality products will be able to sell many of these in the EC and make good profits. This is why it is important for our modern designers to design for people throughout Europe, not just in Britain.

Of course, the other eleven countries will also be trying to sell more of their products in Britain. British products will have to be well designed if they are going to compete.

TOURISM

Many visitors from abroad, especially from Europe, come to Britain every year. Tourism is one of Britain's most important industries. It is still growing. Many visitors come to see the famous sights of London and others want to visit different parts of the country. Buildings from our industrial past are popular attractions.

If we are to make visitors feel welcome, and attract them back for further visits, we must offer them a good service. One way of giving them good service will be to produce well-designed information sheets in their own language. Perhaps we also need to display attractive products for them to buy.

DESIGN TASK

★ Design a symbol to place on a building which shows visitors that they can get advice in their own language inside.

◆ Investigate the range of gifts which visitors to your area can buy. Can you improve on what is available?

◆ Investigate the leaflets published for visitors. Can they be simplified, using more drawings, for people who do not speak English?

★ Design a symbol to show visitors that they can buy unleaded petrol at a garage.

SUCCESS IN EUROPE

The image of a product is very important, as this book has shown. Good first impressions often enable us to win people's attention and goodwill. It is well worth the effort to design and make products to high standards of quality. The single European market should be very good for business, but only in those companies with good designers. These designers, and you may well become one, will have to know about the needs of Europeans. This will be a difficult challenge for many of us but it offers an exciting opportunity. Will *you* accept the challenge to strive for quality?

INDEX

abstraction 11
advertising 6

brainstorming 10, 17, 37
bubble packaging 21
bubble raft 35
bubbles 35

cardboard engineering 31
colour 11, 19, 23
commerce 6
commercial packaging 29
communicator 10
company identity 7, 8
computer 17, 34
containers 26
corroding 32
cost 23, 27
customers 6, 7

design group 10
design source 34
display 6, 7, 8, 11, 12, 14, 16, 17, 22, 27, 44, 45, 47
display cards 15
display unit 22, 23

environment 36
Europe 17, 46, 47
European Community 46
exhibition 45
export 46

folder 42
functional packaging 30, 31

geometrical shapes 34, 35
graphic design 31
graphics 10, 26, 45

image 6, 9, 10, 11, 16, 17, 18, 23, 26, 32, 38, 42, 46
industry 6

lettering 9, 17, 18, 43
litter 28
logo 8, 9, 11, 42, 43

management 7
marketing 16
market research 10
mass production 34
mechanism 33
mini-enterprise project 23, 29
mock-ups 10, 11, 23
mounting 45

natural geometry 34
nature 34
nature's packages 35

packaging 16, 20, 21, 23, 24, 26, 27, 28, 29, 30, 31, 32, 33, 34, 35
photocopies 18, 19
point of sale displays 15, 16

pollution 36
presentation 32, 38, 40, 42, 44, 46
product image 17
products 26
profit 16, 23, 46
prototype 23

quality 16, 42, 47

recycling 37
research 33

scrap 37
shrink wrapping 20, 21
style 33
support card 18
suspension packaging 20, 21
symbol 8, 9, 11, 47
symmetry 45

team work 7
template 19, 21, 34
tessellations 35
tourism 47

vacuum forming 21
value for money 47

waste 36, 37
wealth 16

Acknowledgements

All photography by **Chris Honeywell** with the exception of **Rowntree Mackintosh**, p 32; **Salford Museum and Art Gallery**, p 32; **Reading Museum and Art Gallery**, p 32; **Carole Gutteridge**, p 33; **Telegraph Colour Library**, p 36; **I Keill**, p 47; **Wigan Tourist Office**, p 47.

The publishers would like to acknowledge the help and assistance given by the following: **Access; Boots the Chemist**, Cornmarket Street, Oxford; **Lewis's**, Oxford; **Oxford and Swindon Cooperative Society; Paperchase; Shell UK; Sweet Box; York Castle Museum**.

Illustrations by **Peter Campbell, Diane Fisher, Sarah Nicholson, Lynne Riding**.

Oxford University Press, Walton Street, Oxford OX2 6DP

Oxford New York Toronto
Delhi Bombay Calcutta Madras Karachi
Petaling Jaya Singapore Hong Kong Tokyo
Nairobi Dar es Salaam Cape Town
Melbourne Auckland

and associated companies in
Berlin Ibadan

Oxford is a trade mark of Oxford University Press

© Anne Ablay, Peter Goulden, Neil Nuckley, Peter Toft.

ISBN 0 19 832782 X

Typeset in Garamond light & News Gothic by Tradespools Limited, Frome, Somerset
Printed in Hong Kong

First published 1990